Bill

by Tamera Williams
illustrated by Laura Logan

Core Decodable 18

Bothell, WA • Chicago, IL • Columbus, OH • New York, NY

MHEonline.com

Copyright © 2015 McGraw-Hill Education

All rights reserved. No part of this publication may be reproduced or distributed in any form or by any means, or stored in a database or retrieval system, without the prior written consent of McGraw-Hill Education, including, but not limited to, network storage or transmission, or broadcast for distance learning.

Send all inquiries to:
McGraw-Hill Education
8787 Orion Place
Columbus, OH 43240

ISBN: 978-0-02-145096-1
MHID: 0-02-145096-X

Printed in the United States of America.

2 3 4 5 6 7 8 9 DOC 20 19 18 17 16 15

Pam and Bob hop past Bill.

Bill did not hop.

"Hop, Bill!" said Pam.

"I am hot," said Bill.

Sam and Tom spin past Bill.

Bill did not spin.

"Spin, Bill," said Sam.

"I am still hot," said Bill.

Dot and Al tap past Bill.

Bill did not tap.

"Tap, Bill," said Dot.

"I am hot, hot, hot!" said Bill.

"I am not hot!" said Bill.

"I can hop, spin, and tap!"